DAVID WILLIAMSON is Australia's best-known and most widely performed playwright. His first full-length play, *The Coming of Stork*, was presented at La Mama Theatre in 1970 and was followed by *The Removalists, Don's Party, The Department, The Club, Travelling North, The Perfectionist, Sons of Cain, Emerald City, Top Silk, Money and Friends, Brilliant Lies, Sanctuary, Dead White Males, After the Ball, Corporate Vibes, Face to Face, Rupert, Nearer the Gods, Odd Man Out, Sorting out Rachel, The Big Time,* and *Family Values*. He has had over fifty plays produced. His plays have been translated into many languages and performed internationally, including major productions in London, Los Angeles, New York and Washington. As a screenwriter, Williamson has brought his own plays to the screen, including *The Removalists, Don's Party, The Club, Travelling North* and *Emerald City*, along with his original sscreenplays for feature films, including *Libido, Petersen, Gallipoli, Phar Lap, The Year of Living Dangerously* and *Balibo*. The adaptation of his play *Face to Face*, directed by Michael Rymer, won the Panavision Spirit Award for Independent Film at the Santa Barbara International Film Festival. Williamson was the first person outside Britain to receive the George Devine Award (for *The Removalists*). His many awards include twelve Australian Writers' Guild AWGIE Awards, five Australian Film Institute Awards for Best Screenplay, and in 1996 the United Nations Association of Australia Media Peace Award. In 2005 he was awarded the Richard Lane Award for services to the Australian Writers' Guild. In 2011 he was given the lifetime achievement award by the Sydney Critics Circle. In 2015 he was awarded the NSW Premier's Literary Awards special achievement award. In 2021 his memoir, *Home Truths*, was published by Harper Collins. David has received four honorary doctorates, been made an Officer of the Order of Australia and named one of Australia's Living National Treasures. He lives on Queensland's Sunshine Coast with his writer wife, Kristin Williamson.

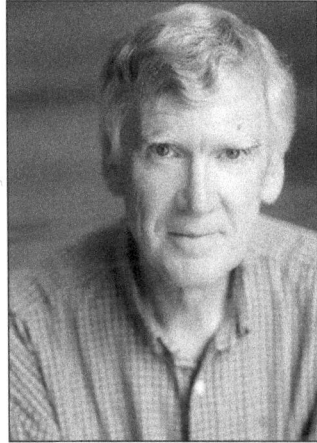

TRAVELLING NORTH

David Williamson

CURRENCY PRESS
The performing arts publisher

CURRENCY PLAYS

First published in 1980
by Currency Press Pty Ltd,
PO Box 2287, Strawberry Hills, NSW, 2012, Australia
enquiries@currency.com.au
www.currency.com.au

This edition published 2022

Copyright: *Travelling North* © David Williamson, 1979, 1980, 2022

Typeset by Integral for Currency Press
Cover design by Lisa White for Currency Press

A catalogue record for this
book is available from the
National Library of Australia

Contents

Currency Press acknowledges the Traditional Owners of the Country on which we live and work. We pay our respects to all Aboriginal and Torres Strait Islander Elders, past and present.

Travelling North was first presented at the Nimrod Theatre, Sydney, on 22 August 1979, with the following cast:

FRANK	Frank Wilson
FRANCES	Carol Raye
SOPHIE	Julie Hamilton
HELEN	Jennifer Hagan
FREDDY	Graham Rouse
SAUL	Henri Szeps
JOAN	Deborah Kennedy
CELEBRANT	Anthony Ingersent
GALLERY ATTENDANT	Deborah Kennedy

Directed by John Bell
Set designed by Ian Robinson

CHARACTERS

FRANCES

FRANK

SOPHIE, Frances' daughter

HELEN, Frances' daughter

JOAN, Frank's daughter

FREDDY WICKS

SAUL MORGENSTEIN

WEDDING CELEBRANT

GALLERY ATTENDANT

SETTING

The action of the play takes place in various locations in North Queensland, Melbourne, an area near Tweed Heads, and Sydney, between 1969 and 1972.

ACT ONE

SCENE ONE

Queensland, late afternoon. The atmosphere is warm and tropical.
FRANCES, *a slim, attractive woman of about fifty-five, wearing an elegantly casual Balinese dress, stands looking outwards, listening.* FRANK *enters. He is a tall, athletic looking man who, although he is over seventy, still exudes energy and vitality. He is wearing neat shorts, long white socks and a pressed silk shirt.* FRANCES *is absorbed in her thoughts and does not hear* FRANK*'s approach. When he speaks she is startled, and her reaction speaks of an underlying tension and anxiety, a characteristic temperamental trait which contrasts with* FRANK*'s assertive air of confidence.*

FRANK: Can you hear the little puffing billies out there hauling in the sugar cane?

FRANCES: I was just listening.

FRANK: They'll keep going all day and all through the night. Sorry I've been away so long, but there's a chap over there with the same model campervan as ours so I struck up a conversation so I could see how he's fitted it out inside.

FRANCES: Did you see anything interesting?

FRANK: No, and I had to listen to half an hour of homespun wisdom before I could get out again. The number of folk philosophers north of the New South Wales border has almost reached plague proportions.

FRANCES: The man we met yesterday came over and invited us for a meal.

> FRANK *begins setting up two deckchairs.*

FRANK: Yes, he stopped me just a second ago, but I saw the lump of cold sausage on the table behind him and politely declined.

> *He takes a pencil, a notebook and a small slide rule from his pocket and begins to make some calculations.*

Five gallons at Noosa gives us a total of eighty-five gallons over a distance of one thousand five hundred and twenty miles, giving us a miles-per-gallon figure of... [*manipulating the slide rule and frowning*] just under eighteen. That damn salesman looked me straight in the eye and said we'd get twenty-three. Naked dishonesty is becoming commonplace.

FRANCES: Still, aside from that it's been a very satisfactory van.

FRANK *continues to manipulate his slide rule.*

And it's been a wonderful holiday. Do you realise we've known each other over a year now and this is the first time we've spent more than a weekend together?

FRANK: Because of this young man's deception, we are running nearly twelve dollars over our petrol budget. I should've checked independent road tests. Why the hell did I ever trust him?

FRANCES: He seemed very honest.

FRANK: A sure sign that he was a crook. It might seem a small matter to you, Frances, but it does take the edge off a trip when you know you've been cheated at the outset. [*Pause.*] I've been thinking a lot about where we should settle, and I think we should go right up into the tropics north of Townsville.

FRANCES: Yes, it would be lovely, but I don't know if I'd like to be quite so far away from my family.

FRANK: If you want my opinion, the further you get away from those daughters of yours the better.

FRANCES: I'm sorry they're behaving in such a surly manner. I really didn't expect it.

FRANK: Neither did I. When I came to pick you up they treated me as if I was a travelling rep for the white slave trade.

FRANCES: I think they're a little embarrassed that technically we're living in sin.

FRANK: By whose standards?

FRANCES: Their standards.

FRANK: By their standards we're living in absolute sin, there's nothing technical about it. But I wouldn't be too sure that the moral question is at the core of it. I think the real reason they're annoyed is that you're not down there to do their housekeeping and babysitting.

FRANCES: Frank!

FRANK: If there was a law against exploiting parents, your two would get ten years apiece. When they learn that we're going to leave Melbourne and live up here permanently they're going to scream blue bloody murder, so be warned and don't let them intimidate you.

FRANCES: How are your children going to react?

FRANK: Well, Eric hasn't spoken to me for fifteen years so I don't think he's going to care much, and I'm sure Joan won't mind, but for heaven's sake let's stop worrying about what our children think. It's our lives, after all.

FRANCES: The girls have been very kind to me, but I must admit I'm getting a bit tired of all their problems and I'm looking forward to us being together by ourselves.

FRANK: It's going to be wonderful, my dear. We're going to lead the ideal life. We'll read, fish, laze, love and lie in the sun.

FRANCES: You make it sound wonderful.

FRANK: It will be.

FRANCES: But we'll still travel?

FRANK: All over the North. We'll use the cottage as a base.

FRANCES: I always get restless if I stay too long in the one spot, no matter how beautiful it is.

FRANK: We'll travel all over the North. You've had a hard struggle bringing up those daughters of yours and it's time you started enjoying life. I'll go and cook the fish.

FRANCES: I'll do that.

FRANK: Indeed you won't. You're my companion, not my slave, and that's the way it's going to stay.

They kiss.

SCENE TWO

Melbourne, winter. It is damp and cold.

SOPHIE *and* HELEN *are talking. Both are very attractive women.* HELEN *is in her late twenties and* SOPHIE *about thirty. They are stylishly dressed in a conventional middle-class manner.* HELEN *is the more direct and incisive of the two. She has an almost neurotic compulsion to ferret out the facts that suggests an underlying suspicion and resentment of the world in general.* SOPHIE *seems gentler, more well-adjusted, but there is a quality of self-absorption about her that often causes her to lose concentration on the immediate proceedings and withdraw into her own thoughts.*

SOPHIE: It sounds as though it's really what she wants.

HELEN: She wouldn't know what she wants. She's the original reed who's blown around in the wind. Frank has pressured her into it. I knew the old fox was working away at something.

SOPHIE: I still think she really wants to go.

HELEN: He's an old man who needs someone to look after him and she'll just be used up. The trouble with Mother is that she just never, never, never thinks ahead.

SOPHIE: Try and be a bit generous, Helen. They're like two teenagers in love and it's rather sweet.

HELEN: I think it's nauseating.

SOPHIE: They've been sending each other two letters a day. Even at the height of adol-escence I couldn't match that sort of enthusiasm.

HELEN: I think the whole thing's sick. Falling in love is what you do when you're eighteen. They should be old enough to know better.

SCENE THREE

The same setting, some time later.

FRANCES *is being interrogated by her two daughters.*

SOPHIE: We're very glad for you, Mother. Really.

HELEN: It's your life. You're entitled to do exactly what you want with it.

FRANCES: Frank wanted to go right up north, but we've settled for Tweed Heads so I'll be able to fly to Melbourne. I'll probably be down here as often as I'm up there.

SOPHIE: If that's what you want, then we're very happy for you.

FRANCES: The winter climate is so much better up there and as you get older the climate seems to become more and more important.

HELEN: You realise, of course, that the summer up there is unbearably sticky.

FRANCES: Yes, I do rather prefer our dry summers down here.

HELEN: I'm really very happy for you, Mother, and I don't want you to think I'm playing the devil's advocate, but you have thought all this through, haven't you?

FRANCES: Oh, yes.

HELEN: You do realise that a six-week trip may be a different proposition than living with Frank full-time?

FRANCES: What do you mean?

SOPHIE: From what I've seen of him, Frank can be pretty dogmatic and assertive.

FRANCES: I'm aware of his faults.

SOPHIE: And he's nearly twenty years older than you are.

FRANCES: He's very fit and his brain is as agile as a twenty-year-old.

HELEN: He's not going to stay that way forever and we don't want to see you ending up as a full-time nursemaid. He's very sick at the moment, isn't he?

FRANCES: He caught a heavy cold when we came back to Melbourne, but—

HELEN: Pneumonia, according to what you told Sophie.

FRANCES: Yes, but he's had penicillin and he's well over the worst of it.

HELEN: I don't want to sound brutal, Mother, but did it ever occur to you that he might be looking for someone to care for him in his declining years?

FRANCES: You always manage to find the most ugly motives in quite wonderful things, Helen. We've fallen in love and we want to live together. I'm sorry I'm leaving you both because I know it's a very hectic time in both your lives and I liked to feel I was helping out in some small way...

SOPHIE: We're not upset because you won't be around to babysit, Mama, we're upset because we'll miss you. Jim says you're the most un-mother-in-law mother-in-law he could imagine. Quite frankly, I think he enjoys your company better than mine. We just want to be sure you realise the implications of what you're doing because we don't want you to be unhappy.

FRANCES: I appreciate that, dear.

SOPHIE: You have been known to be impulsive and people have taken advantage of you in the past.

HELEN: Is Frank going to marry you?

FRANCES: I don't think so. He doesn't really believe in it.

SOPHIE: How do you feel about that?

FRANCES: I'd be lying if I said I was entirely happy. Logically I can see that if two people love each other a certificate isn't necessary, but I was brought up in a religious family and it's hard to get rid of all the residual guilt.

HELEN: You realise, of course, that if you aren't married you've got no legal protection whatsoever. When he dies you might get nothing in his will.

FRANCES: Those sort of things don't really worry me. Besides, he's got very little to bequeath.

HELEN: What are you going to live on?

FRANCES: Frank's got a little bit of superannuation and we'll have his pension.

HELEN: That won't be enough.

FRANCES: We're going to live very simply.

SOPHIE: Won't you be isolated up there, Mama? You won't be able to go to films, theatre, galleries… all the things you love.

FRANCES: We'll be near enough to Sydney to go down there quite often.

HELEN: How will you afford it?

FRANCES: We'll manage.

HELEN: I think you should absolutely insist that he marries you.

FRANCES: I couldn't.

HELEN: Why not?

FRANCES: He doesn't believe in it and I'm afraid I just don't feel strongly enough about it to make a fuss.

HELEN: Sometimes you should make a fuss, Mama. That's your trouble. You never face things squarely.

SCENE FOUR

The same setting, some time later.

SOPHIE *and* HELEN *are alone.*

HELEN: Did you know they had sex the second time they met?

SOPHIE: How did you know that?

HELEN: I read their letters.

SOPHIE: Helen, you shouldn't read Mama's mail.

HELEN: I know, but I did.

SOPHIE: I thought they'd be past all that.

HELEN: You should read them. They're revolting. 'Eager bodies pressing down' and all that sort of nonsense. People of that age ought to have better things to do with their time. Did you know he was a Communist?

SOPHIE: No, he isn't. He resigned from the Party after Hungary.

HELEN: We built that whole new room onto the house two years ago so that Mama had somewhere to stay. It cost us a fortune and it's all totally wasted.

SOPHIE: That's not—

HELEN: Well, quite frankly, I'm really irritated. She's acted on impulse and whim all her life—

SOPHIE: Helen—

HELEN: She has. She's always been erratic and irresponsible.

SOPHIE: Erratic perhaps, but I wouldn't say irresponsible.

HELEN: You weren't shot off to live with your uncle when you were only eight.

SOPHIE: She was having a hard time.

HELEN: There were a lot of other divorced mothers having a hard time who didns't farm out their kids. I'm sorry, but the truth of the matter is that she couldn't be bothered with us then, and she still can't be bothered with us now.

SCENE FIVE

Melbourne. It is cold and wintry.

FRANK, *dressed in a neat pullover and slacks, talks to* JOAN, *an attractive and intelligent woman in her early thirties.*

FRANK: I just thought I'd let you know.

JOAN: I'm very happy for you. I like Frances a lot.

FRANK: We're not getting married.

He sneezes.

JOAN: That's no surprise.

FRANK: This damn chill, sodden Melbourne wind will kill me if I stay down here another winter. You're not upset at this decision, are you?

JOAN: Why should I be upset?

FRANK: Some children apparently get upset when their parents start a new relationship. They see it as an act of betrayal against the memory of the other parent.

JOAN: Mum's been dead a long while now.

FRANK: I think you're mature enough to realise that nothing will ever tarnish the affection and fond memories I had of your mother. We were in some ways, I think, the perfect married couple.

JOAN: Come on.

FRANK: What's that supposed to mean?

JOAN: I don't know whether Mother would have agreed with that if she was still around.

FRANK: Why do you say that?

JOAN: Just joking.

FRANK: We had our differences, but your mother was a fine woman and I loved her very much. Have you heard from your brother recently?

JOAN: Very little.

FRANK: I presume he still has no desire to communicate with me, so you'll tell him about this, will you?

JOAN: I will.

FRANK: Are you still friendly with that self-opinionated popinjay who talks too fast and hasn't got a brain in his head?

JOAN: Yes I am, and I think I should tell you that he's got a similarly high opinion of you.

FRANK: Are you living with him yet?

JOAN: No.

FRANK: He doesn't deserve you. How are things at work?

JOAN: Good. The school's swung over to open-classroom teaching and I'm enjoying it.

FRANK: Is that the system where the kids do what they like?

JOAN: They work on projects of their own choice.

FRANK: Doomed to failure. You'll turn out a mob of anarchist illiterates.

JOAN: I thought you were supposed to be a progressive thinker.

FRANK: Socialism and discipline aren't incompatible, my dear.

JOAN: Well, we can forget socialism now that Gorton's in.

FRANK: Don't give up. We'll win in seventy-two. That terrible daughter of Frances's is coming to see me.

JOAN: Sophie? She's quite nice.

FRANK: No, the tough one with the sharp tongue and a mind like a steel trap.

JOAN: Oh, Helen. Yes, she is pretty formidable.

FRANK: She's coming to blast me for spiriting off her mother, and quite frankly I'm terrified.

SCENE SIX

Melbourne. It is cold and bleak.

HELEN *is talking to* FRANK. FRANK *is clearly nervous.*

FRANK: More tea?

HELEN: No, thanks.

FRANK: Biscuits?

HELEN: No, thanks.

FRANK: So your mother's told you about our plans?

HELEN: Yes, she has.

FRANK: Very good of you to come and discuss things.

HELEN: I thought perhaps we should talk to each other before you left.

FRANK: Frances is very sad to be moving away from you.

HELEN: It's going to be a wrench for us all.

FRANK: It's just, I suppose, that she's reached the time of life where she wants to put her own interests first.

HELEN: I'm not quite sure that she knows what her own interests are.

FRANK: I think you do her an injustice.

HELEN: I just wondered if you were fully aware of just what exactly she is giving up by this move.

FRANK: She's been very happy down here. There's no doubt about that, and she's become very, very fond of all your children. How is young Tarquin, by the way?

HELEN: Tarquin is one of Sophie's children.

FRANK: Of course, how stupid of me. Yours is, er…

HELEN: I've got three.

FRANK: Yes but, er, isn't there one with a name like Tarquin?

HELEN: No, nothing like Tarquin. In my opinion Tarquin is a pretentious, dated and rather stupid name, but that's Sophie's business. The child you're probably referring to is called Tobias.

FRANK: Ah, yes. Tobias.

HELEN: I just wondered if you were fully aware, for instance, that Mother has a fully furnished room set aside for her at both of our houses, that she is free to come and go at any time, that she is never allowed, although to her credit she tries, to pay any money towards her upkeep, and that aside from a little babysitting here and there she is able to see as many concerts, plays, films and exhibitions as she needs.

FRANK: She's been very happy down here, but she feels now...

HELEN: The Melbourne weather apparently doesn't meet with your approval, but this is, for all its faults, the cultural capital of the nation, a fact that Mother, with her plethora of cultural interests, has relished, so you see when you said that she's putting her own interests first, and when you suggest travelling up north to a steamy, isolated, little shack with someone who, to be polite, has seen the best years of his life, I wonder whether you have really seriously considered what it is you're doing?

FRANK: Are you suggesting that I'm spiriting her up there against her will?

HELEN: Mother is a very impressionable woman. In any given situation she tends to follow the loudest voice.

FRANK: In that case she would certainly stay down here with you. Now if you've finished your tea I'd like to go on my daily walk.

SCENE SEVEN

The new cottage.

We know immediately we are near the tropics by the changes in lighting and scenery. A first glimpse of the place shows it to be a wreck. FRANCES is cleaning rubbish from the cupboards and piling it on the floor. The door opens and FRANK enters in a shirt and shorts. Vivaldi is heard on the radio in the background.

FRANK: This bedroom is a hideous mess. I asked the agent to have the place cleaned out.

FRANCES: I couldn't care if it was ten times as bad. We're here and we're together and I'm very happy.

FRANK: So am I. It's like a junkyard after a cyclone. How could anyone have lived in this?

FRANCES: The garden is wonderful. Hibiscus, frangipani, poinsettias and there's even a marvellous little banana plant, and there are pink angophoras by the thousands on the hill behind us.

FRANK: Yes, it's a good little spot.

FRANCES: I've never heard so many bellbirds.

FRANK: Yes, it's a regular little paradise. The edge of the lake is thick with black swans and ibis.

FRANCES: It's very, very beautiful.

FRANK: And the best part about it all is that there isn't another house in sight.

FREDDY: [*offstage*] Anyone at home?

> FRANK *goes to the door.* FREDDY, *a jovial man in his sixties enters, wearing a bright shirt and shorts.*

G'day there. Am I intruding?

FRANK: No. I, er, don't believe we've met?

FREDDY: Freddy Wicks, your neighbour. I saw you'd arrived so I came across to see if I could lend a hand.

FRANK: That's very kind of you. I'm Frank and this is Frances.

FRANCES: I didn't realise we had a neighbour, Mr Wicks.

FREDDY: Freddy, please. No, you can't see me from here. I'm up the back there into the trees, so cheer up, you're not on your own after all.

FRANK: [*dully*] What a surprise.

FRANCES: Are you there by yourself?

FREDDY: Yeah. Ever since I lost the wife eight years ago.

FRANCES: I am sorry.

FREDDY: Yeah. A happy marriage. A blameless life. Snuffed out like a candle. Makes you wonder.

FRANCES: Have you any children?

FREDDY: Yep. Two boys and a girl. They've all done well: one's a teacher, one's a lawyer and m'daughter married a Qantas pilot, but it gets a bit lonely up there all by m'self. But let's not be morbid. Would you like an ale?

> *He deposits two beer bottles on a table.*

FRANK: Well, perhaps a bit later. We're trying to clean this rubbish out.

FREDDY: I've got a ute up there. I'll bring it down and help you cart the stuff to the tip. I don't want to sound like a snob, but it's a great relief to have an educated couple like yourselves in here. I'm not saying anything against old Sam, God rest his soul, but he wasn't the sort of neighbour you could have an informed discussion with.

FRANK: He died here, I take it.

FREDDY: Yes, right there where you're standing. I was the one who found him. The poor bugger drank himself to death. The climate here's fine, but I find that if you don't keep your mind active you can get a bit morbid. Where do you two come from?

FRANK: Melbourne.

FREDDY: I had a cousin from Melbourne. Poor fellow shot himself.

FRANK: It can have that effect on you.

FREDDY: How long have you two been together?

FRANK: If you mean under the same roof, about an hour and a half.

FREDDY: Have you just married?

FRANK: No. We're living in sin.

FREDDY: Go on.

FRANK: You've got a ute, you say?

FREDDY: Yes, I could back in up the drive.

FRANK: That's very kind of you. The sooner we shift this junk out the better.

SCENE EIGHT

FRANK *and* FRANCES *sit in the cottage garden at twilight.*

FRANK: Well, my love, we've got no water supply other than the rain, no sewerage, no mail, milk or paper delivery, no rubbish collection, no bitumen on the road, and Freddy, but we are right in the middle of subtropical splendour at its very best and we have got each other.

FRANCES: You've been a bit cruel to poor Freddy. He seems a good soul at heart.

FRANK: He is, he is. A no-nonsense, salt-of-the-earth, plain-speaking, straight-talking, nosy, interfering, moralistic, insensitive… Do you find the township depressing?

FRANCES: No, I think it's lovely. I didn't expect so many trees.

FRANK: No! The people! Bald, sunburnt heads, pink faces and fat bellies. they look as if they've been interbreeding with the local crayfish.

FREDDY *comes down into the garden.*

FREDDY: Evening.

FRANCES: Hello, Freddy. Thanks for helping us clean everything up.

FRANK: [*reluctantly*] Yes, thanks.

FREDDY: No worries. If you can't help your neighbours now and then you might as well live in a cave. You weren't a serviceman by any chance, Frank?

FRANK: I was, as a matter of fact. In both wars.

FREDDY: There's one of the best RSL clubs along the coast down in the township. Why don't you and Frances come down with me and I'll introduce you around?

FRANK: Not just tonight, thanks all the same, Freddy.

FREDDY: You can get a solid three-course meal and a floorshow straight up from Sydney for just over five dollars.

FRANK: Sounds very good value, but not just tonight.

FREDDY: It's not just a boozers' club. We have discussion nights and everything.

FRANK: Discussion nights?

FREDDY: We had the federal vice-president up last Friday night tearing strips off those Vietnam protesters.

FRANK: Why was he doing that?

FREDDY: Because they're marching in support of the enemy while our lads are out there dying in the jungle and that's near enough to treason in my book.

FRANK: Have you ever asked yourself what our lads are doing out there in someone else's jungles, Freddy?

FREDDY: They're trying to stop a Communist takeover.

FRANK: That's a load of twaddle, Freddy.

FRANCES: I know how you feel, Freddy, but I really don't think this is a war we should be proud of.

FRANK: There's no war anyone can be proud of.

FREDDY: I fought against Hitler and I'm proud of that.

FRANK: This war is different, Freddy. Use your brains, man. Think! Don't go around parroting platitudes like, 'My country right or wrong'. It's nonsense!

FREDDY. Everyone's entitled to their opinion, Frank. [*Pause.*] I'd better be making tracks.

FRANCES: Thanks again for your help, Freddy.

FREDDY: If you need me again, just call. We mightn't see eye to eye on everything but I think you'll find I'm a good neighbour.

SCENE NINE

A doctor's surgery.

SAUL MORGENSTEIN, *sallow, lugubrious, manic depressive, wry, in his sixties, sits behind his desk.* FRANK *enters.*

SAUL: Mr Frank Brown?

FRANK: That's right.

SAUL: My name is Saul Morgenstein. You're new to the district.

FRANK: Comparatively. I've been here two months.

SAUL: I've been here eight years and I'm still regarded as a newcomer. Do you like the area?

FRANK: It's very beautiful.

SAUL: It is, isn't it? And very peaceful. I've had an interesting life, Mr Brown. In fact my life has been so interesting that I can scarcely believe I've had it, but at this end all I want is tranquillity. What's your problem?

FRANK: No real problem. I'd just like a check-up.

SAUL: You have a check-up regularly?

FRANK: Not really. I just thought it was about time I did.

SAUL: When some people ask for a check-up it usually means that something more specific is worrying them.

FRANK: As far as I know I'm in excellent health.

SAUL: [*taking* FRANK*'s blood pressure*] Do you like fishing?

FRANK: Yes, I love fishing.

SAUL: Did that crooked estate agent Foulmouth tell you that the fishing in the lake was excellent?

FRANK: Falmont? Yes, he did.

SAUL: He's a liar. He did the same thing to me. The lake looks magnificent, but the bottom is choked with weed. If he ever gets piles I'll prescribe mustard-coated suppositories. What do you do for a living, Mr Brown?

FRANK: I was a civil engineer. I also led an active life in politics.

SAUL: Did you ever run for office?

FRANK: Yes, I did.

SAUL: Did you win?

FRANK: No. It's quite hard when you're the candidate in Toorak.

SAUL: When did you do this?

FRANK: In the thirties.

SAUL: Not a very popular time to be a Communist, I imagine.

FRANK: No it wasn't, and I paid for it.

SAUL: How?

FRANK: In cash. The construction firm I worked for sacked me at fifty-nine and I only got a fraction of my superannuation entitlements.

SAUL: Stand up, please.

FRANK: Have you any scruples about examining an ex-Communist?

SAUL: Not at all. I'm much more worried about the lack of superannuation.

FRANK: I'm insured.

SAUL: I saw you in the township yesterday with a lady. Was that your wife?

FRANK: Yes.

SAUL: There's some talk in the township that she isn't. Legally.

FRANK: She isn't, legally.

SAUL: She's a very attractive woman.

FRANK: [a trifle terse] Yes, she is.

SAUL: I'm sorry about all the questions, Mr Brown, but I think we'll be seeing a lot more of each other in future so I'd like to get past formalities.

FRANK: Why will we be seeing a lot more of each other?

SAUL: When you were walking down the main street yesterday you stopped and leaned against a post.

FRANK: I had pneumonia in Melbourne last year and ever since I often get short of breath.

SAUL: After exercise?

FRANK: Yes.

SAUL: A tightening of the chest?

FRANK: Yes. [Pause.] Is it anything to do with my heart?

SAUL: Yes it is. You're getting mild angina.

FRANK: What does that mean exactly?

SAUL: It means that your heart muscle and arteries have deteriorated to some degree and can't supply the heart with enough blood during and after exercise. Hence the chest pains and breathlessness.

FRANK: Can you be certain that's what it is?

SAUL: No. I can send you to Sydney for a cardiograph if you like, but the symptoms are very clear.

FRANK: What are my long-term chances?

SAUL: You're not going to make a hundred, Mr Brown. Can I call you Frank?

FRANK: Please do.

SAUL: But if you take the right drugs and take things easily then there's every chance you'll go on for years and years.

FRANK: How many years?

SAUL: I can't give you an exact figure. It could be three, five, ten, even longer.

FRANK: As little as three?

SAUL: Look, you could drop dead tomorrow. I don't think you will, in fact I wouldn't mind betting you'll outlive me, but in a case like this there's no way of knowing.

FRANK: I see.

SAUL: We are very imperfect machines, Frank, and we wear out. If there is a creator somewhere I can't help feeling he went on to better things on some other planet. My problem is ulcers. I have to live on biscuits and milk.

FRANK: Better those than a weak heart.

SAUL: You'd feel differently after a few weeks of biscuits and milk. There's very little joy in growing old.

FRANK: What does this illness mean in terms of alteration to my life patterns?

SAUL: I've told you already. You take things easy.

FRANK: What about the, hmm, intimate areas?

SAUL: Intimate areas? Are you still…?

FRANK: I am old, but I am not defunct.

SAUL: Well, er, if you've been managing up to now, by all means keep trying. Angina in a sense is like having your own built-in doctor. Whenever you feel pain, stop what you're doing and try again later. This may prove disconcerting to your good wife, but remind her of the words of Lord Wellington: that a strategic withdrawal is often the first step towards a forward thrust of renewed vigour. I'll write you out some prescriptions.

SCENE TEN

The cottage interior. It is night.

FRANK *is reading the paper.* FRANCES *is restless.*

FRANK: Are you going to church again this Sunday?

FRANCES: I'd like to.

FRANK: You puzzle me, Frances. You're obviously an intelligent woman, and your political stance, while not being terribly radical, is at least decently progressive, but your respect for religion has me puzzled.

FRANCES: I'm sorry, Frank, but I just can't shake off my belief that there's a God.

FRANK: How can there by a God, my love? This world is so full of misery and injustice that it's beyond credulity to think that it was all organised by a loving Father.

FRANCES: It might be illogical but I just believe in him, Frank.

FRANK: Do you pray?

FRANCES: Yes. Quite often.

FRANK: Do you think he objects to us not being married?

FRANCES: I think he'd prefer it if we were.

FRANK: My dear Frances, whom I love dearly, do you really think that God, with billions of people to look after on this planet alone, is really losing sleep over the fact that an old geriatric on the New South Wales coast is cohabiting out of wedlock with a much younger lady?

FRANCES: It isn't logical or rational, but I just feel that he knows and cares.

FRANK: Then he's an old busybody.

Pause. FRANCES *paces restlessly.*

FRANCES: Do you think it's time we loaded the van and went up north?

FRANK: We've hardly settled in here.

FRANCES: We've been here over six months.

FRANK: The fish are really biting in the lake at the moment. Why don't you come out with me in the boat?

FRANCES: I don't really enjoy it, Frank.

FRANK: Well, stay here and read a book.

FRANCES: I can't concentrate. I know it's silly of me but I just can't concentrate. I have to put the book down and go for a walk. Can we go down to Sydney?

FRANK: Sydney? What do you want to go to that polluted hole for when we're up here in one of the most beautiful places on God's earth?

FRANCES: I'd like to see some exhibitions and some theatre.

FRANK: It's such an exhausting business organising the whole thing that it's hardly worth doing. Who was the letter from?

FRANCES: Helen.

FRANK: How is she?

FRANCES: Fine. Sophie is going to have a baby.

FRANK: Another one?

FRANCES: It's come at a very bad time for her because of her studies.

FRANK: Hmm.

FRANCES: I thought perhaps we could go down to Melbourne then.

FRANK: When's it due?

FRANCES: August.

FRANK: August. That's in the middle of winter. I'm not going down there in August.

FRANCES: It's a little hard to reschedule the baby at this stage. If you feel you don't want to come, I can go by myself.

FRANK: If you go down there by yourself those damn daughters of yours will chain you up and not let you back.

FRANCES: Don't be silly.

FRANK: Why are you so edgy lately?

FRANCES: Well, my daily routine is not all that exciting. I watch you out on the lake all morning, I get a lecture from Freddy on why our boys should be in Vietnam in the afternoon, I cook the evening meal then get a lecture from you on why they shouldn't be in Vietnam at night. You've changed, Frank. You used to love to travel.

FRANK: You're right. We mustn't stagnate. As soon as I've got this lung trouble under control we'll go down south for the baby.

FRANCES: The lung trouble is nothing serious, is it?

FRANK: No. It's just an aftermath of the pneumonia.

FRANCES: If it was something more serious, you wouldn't try to hide it from me, would you?

FRANK: Why would I try and do that, my love?

FRANCES: Because you don't want me to worry about you, and I appreciate that, but really I'd rather know than not know.

FRANK: I've got a slight problem with my heart.

FRANCES: Your heart?

FRANK: It's just a slight deterioration of the heart muscles. It's not really serious at all. Saul says I could live for another fifteen years.

FRANCES: Perhaps we shouldn't drive down to Melbourne.

FRANK: It really isn't all that serious, my love. [Seeing something in the paper] Damn! Graham Byford died.

FRANCES: Graham Byford?

FRANK: You wouldn't know him. He had a property up on Tinaroo Lake. I used to call on him every time I went up there.

FRANCES: How old was he?

FRANK: Seventy-two. The last time I saw him he was fighting fit and walking five miles a day. He should have lived to ninety-five, damn it. He should have lived to ninety-five!

SCENE ELEVEN

Saul's surgery.

FRANK *and* SAUL *are talking.*

FRANK: I'd like to know a bit more about these tablets I'm taking, Saul

SAUL: Have they helped the chest pains?

FRANK: In general, yes, but I've had some pretty sharp ones over the last couple of weeks. I've been writing to one of my old friends with a similar condition and the tablets he's taking seem to be quite different from mine.

SAUL: That's quite possible. There are a lot of alternative medications.

FRANK: Just exactly how do the tablets I'm taking at present operate and how do they differ from the other prescriptions available?

SAUL: The Anginine relieves the immediate symptoms during an attack and the Lanoxin tones up your heartstrings.

FRANK: Tones up my heartstrings?

SAUL: In a manner of speaking.

FRANK: Saul, I hope you don't feel I'm being excessively demanding, but I'm starting to find the level of your medical explanation a little unsatisfactory.

SAUL: You don't need to know the details.

FRANK: Listen, Saul, I'm the one who's going to die of this condition, not you, so if you don't mind I'll decide what I need to know and what I don't. How exactly do the two drugs operate, and how do you know that the ones you've chosen are the best in the available range?

SAUL: I don't know exactly how the drugs operate. I'm a general practitioner, not a biochemist.

FRANK: Why did you choose Lanoxin and Anginine?

SAUL: Because they've worked with other patients.

FRANK: Where are all the available drugs listed?

SAUL: In the manuals.

FRANK: Where can I get copies?

SAUL: You can't. They're only available to qualified medical practitioners.

FRANK: That's ridiculous.

SAUL: Why is it ridiculous? If they were freely available every Tom, Dick and Harry would think they knew more than their doctors.

FRANK: If 'toning up the heartstrings' is the best explanation their doctors could offer to explain the effects of a toxic drug on a complex system of musculature, then who would blame them?

SAUL: You can be a very arrogant and irritating man, Frank.

FRANK: I ran a firm which employed seven hundred people, Saul. I won't be treated like a moron. I want a copy of those manuals.

SAUL: Then you'd better go and qualify as a doctor.

FRANK: It's a ridiculous and criminal state of affairs when a man is denied access to information about drugs that are vital to his survival.

SAUL: Frank, will you please go?

FRANK: Why is it that you medicos are so scared of letting your patients know what's going on? Do you just like the sense of power and authority or do you think we'll discover you're a pack of frauds? I want those manuals, Saul, and I'm not leaving here until you tell me how to go about getting them.

SAUL: Calm down or you'll have an attack!

FRANK: Then give me the manuals or I'll have it right here in your surgery and completely foul up your morning!

SAUL: I've got fifteen patients waiting out there.

FRANK: Exactly, so don't let's have a fuss.

SAUL: [grabbing books from the shelf] There you are. Take them! Drug manuals, reference books on heart disease, and if there's anything else you want, take that too. Just take them and get out. You're having an extremely bad effect on my ulcers.

SCENE TWELVE

Melbourne.

HELEN *speaks to* SOPHIE *on the telephone.* SOPHIE *is looking very pregnant.*

HELEN: Have you had a letter from Mother?

SOPHIE: Yes, I got one today.

HELEN: She hasn't written to me for two weeks. You got one last week too, didn't you?

SOPHIE: Yes, but that was because she'd just read some article about healthy diets during pregnancy.

HELEN: Did she say when she was planning to come down?

SOPHIE: Yes, in about three weeks. Frank's coming with her.

HELEN: Why?

SOPHIE: He wants to see his daughter.

HELEN: I thought he was supposed to be sick?

SOPHIE: He is and Mama sounds a little bit worried about bringing him on the trip, because she's found out that he's got some sort of a heart condition.

HELEN: Heart condition. I thought it was lungs?

SOPHIE: Apparently it's heart.

HELEN: Lovely! So she's got a permanent invalid on her hands for the rest of his life. How's the little one? Kicking?

SOPHIE: Like a mule. You're very good sending her money.

HELEN: She sent the first one or two cheques back. But I knew she needed it. That old bastard took the bulk of his superannuation in a lump sum, so he could buy himself a yacht, which he sails around the lake while she peels the spuds. Might be twins. You're very big.

SOPHIE: Don't say that. I couldn't bear the thought.

HELEN: It runs in the family. Our great-uncle was a twin.

SOPHIE: Don't.

HELEN: Eileen Hanrahan had twins and she said it wasn't too bad. She put one on each breast.

SOPHIE: Oh God!

HELEN: I think I might have another bub.

SOPHIE: Are you serious?

HELEN: Yes.

SOPHIE: You said you'd never even consider it. Why have you changed your mind?

HELEN: Moya Simpson's just had another one and it's made me clucky.

SOPHIE: That's not a very good reason.

HELEN: It's not the only one. I actually get a little bit of attention when I'm pregnant. Martin's parents are almost friendly to me from seven months through to the first viewing, and Martin comes to see me in the hospital every second day, which means I see him far more often than normal. He even flew home early from a conference in Surfers Paradise after I had Janessa. The cyclone alert probably had something to do with it too, but I like to think the best of people.

SOPHIE: So I've noticed. Is Martin keen on the idea?

HELEN: Who can tell? He just grunted: 'Fair enough, what's for dinner?' Now it's just a matter of letting nature take its course, which can mean quite a wait in Martin's case. He's quite virile when the firm's sales figures go up, but they're having a very bad year.

SOPHIE: [*laughing*] Stop it.

HELEN: No, it's true. A five percent rise in sales and it's like a second honeymoon, but right now…

She shrugs.

SOPHIE: Count your blessings.

HELEN: If you hear from Mama, tell her I'm still here and still waiting for a letter, will you?

SOPHIE: I'm sure there's one in the post.

SCENE THIRTEEN

The cottage. Day.

FRANK *and* FRANCES *prepare to leave on their journey to Melbourne.* FRANK *checks offstage items packed in a box against a list.*

FRANK: [offstage] Shaving gear, mirror, towels, tracksuits, medicines, pills, cash, transistor, torch, hot water bottles, mosquito coils, camera, double adapter, scissors, whetstone, maps, list of caravan parks, insect repellent, teapot, tin opener, safety pins, sunglasses and slide rule—and, of course, my tablets.

FRANCES: You seem to have an extraordinary number of pills and tablets.

FRANK: [*offstage*] I'm testing which ones are the most effective.

FRANCES: Does Saul let you have as many as you want?

FRANK: [*offstage*] We have an understanding. I test the samples the reps leave.

> FRANCES *brings out a suitcase ready for loading into the van. There is a knock at the door and* FREDDY *enters.*

FREDDY: You're off, then?

FRANK: Yes, we've finally made it.

FREDDY: Have a good trip. Hope everything goes well with the baby.

FRANK: Keep an eye on the place for us, Freddy.

FREDDY: Yeah, I will, and I might just have a little surprise for you when you come back.

FRANK: A surprise?

FREDDY: Yeah. You've got a lovely little garden out there but there's one essential item missing.

FRANK: There is?

FREDDY: How'd you like a barbecue down by your banana plant?

FRANK: A barbecue. By our banana plant. Well, er, that sounds wonderful, but we, er, don't eat all that much meat.

FREDDY: You've got to have a barbecue, Frank. Everyone does up here. It's part of the outdoor living.

FRANCES: It's very kind of you, Freddy, but we really wouldn't want you to go to all that trouble.

FREDDY: It's no trouble, really. I enjoy building things, in fact I've drawn up a plan of it already. If you hang on here a second I'll go and get it.

FRANK: How big is it going to be?

FREDDY: I was thinking of a fairly simple one about so high [*indicating chest level*] but I can make a big one if you'd rather.

FRANK: No, please…

FREDDY: Hang on while I get the plans.

> *He goes outside.*

FRANK: We've got to stop him. We'll load the things in the van so we can say no and run.

He picks up the case and heads for the door, but stops short.

FRANCES: Another pain?

FRANK *nods.*

Sit down. It's a bad one, isn't it?

FRANK: Damn thing. It must have been the thought of Freddy's barbecue.

FRANCES: I'll run up and get Freddy to go for Saul.

FRANK: If this proves serious, there's a letter of instructions in my top drawer.

FRANCES: Frank, you're going to be all right.

FRANK: The first thing I want you to do if I die is to break open a magnum of champagne and share it with Saul and Freddy. Not a bottle, a magnum.

FRANCES *runs out, leaving* FRANK *alone.*

For all my faults I'm damn well worth a magnum.

END OF ACT ONE

ACT TWO

SCENE ONE

The cottage, a short time later.

FRANK *lies in bed propped up by pillows.* FRANCES *brings him a cup of hot beverage.* FRANK *sips it and grimaces.*

FRANK: What's this?

FRANCES: Promite. Saul recommended it.

FRANK: I might have known. It tastes like drain water.

FRANCES: He said it was good for you.

FRANK: What did he tell you when you went outside?

FRANCES: He said you'd have to take things very easily.

FRANK: What else did he say?

FRANCES: He said it was a heart attack but not a very severe one.

FRANK: He told me I could either regard it as a very severe bout of angina or a small heart attack, whichever made me feel happier. He's got a very fatalistic sense of humour. I am afraid, though, that whatever we choose to call it, there's no escaping the fact that it signals the beginning of the end.

FRANCES: Drink your Promite and don't be morbid.

FRANK: I'm just being realistic, and we've got to be, because it does mean that we've got to take stock of our relationship.

FRANCES: No philosophising, Frank. Just rest.

FRANK: We must face up to it. Saul says that what I need to do from here on in is to lead a life of indolence and ease, be thoroughly pampered and have every whim instantly satisfied and I could live forever, but the point is that while that's going to be fine for me it's going to be hell for you, and if you felt like reneging on our pact I wouldn't blame you or be the least bit surprised.

FRANCES: Frank, you're the first man I've ever really loved in my life, and I'm not about to run out on you. Now please drink your Promite and relax.

FRANK: At the very least you mustn't abandon your plans to go down for the birth of the baby.

FRANCES: Stop it.

FRANK: No, really. I can look after myself.

FRANCES: Saul says you're not allowed to move for a week, let alone look after yourself. I can see the baby when it's a bit older. They're ugly little things when they're first born, in any case.

FRANK: They are, I must admit. Red, wrinkled, squawking little sods, and anyone who claims they can tell who the poor thing resembles is either lying or being very insulting to the chosen forebear. Nonetheless, it's something grandparents don't like to miss and I'm sorry you can't be down there, and in all seriousness, when and if looking after me becomes too arduous, I expect you to go.

FRANCES: If you don't stop talking, I'll go straight away.

FRANK: Seriously, though, you're not bound by any marriage vows so I expect you to cry 'Enough' when the time comes.

FRANCES: [agitated] Frank, please stop urging me to run out on you. I dodged my responsibilities when I was younger but I'm not going to do it now.

FRANK: I'm not your responsibility.

FRANCES: [agitated] You are, so please, please stop talking about it!

FRANK: When did you even run out on your responsibilities in the past? You ran a boarding house, you cooked, you cleaned, you did everything you damn well could to keep those kids of yours clothed and fed.

FRANCES: And when the pressure got too much for me I gave them away. I sent Helen off to my brother's for four years when she was only eight. And I don't think she's ever forgiven me.

FRANK: You're the most guilt-prone woman I've ever met. You were under a lot of pressure and you did the best you could.

FRANCES: It wasn't really the financial pressure, Frank. I sent the children away because I simply wanted some time to do the things I wanted to do.

FRANK: Good for you, and when you need some time to do the things you want to do again, then you mustn't hesitate to leave me.

FRANCES: Please stop it, Frank.

FRANK: All right. If you're going to use me as a guinea pig to test your powers of endurance, then your first task is to tip the rest of this indescribable muck down the sink.

FRANCES: It's rich in Vitamin B.

FRANK: You could at least stir it properly.

FRANCES: Sorry.

FRANK: Frances, sometimes I'm an old bastard.

FRANCES: [*ironically*] No!

SCENE TWO

Melbourne, winter.

SOPHIE *is visiting* HELEN. *The new baby is in a carry cot.*

HELEN: He's gorgeous, Sophie, but I'm afraid he's the image of Jim.

SOPHIE: I know. It's totally unfair.

HELEN: It's a pity Mama couldn't come down.

SOPHIE: Mmm. It wasn't a heart attack, apparently. It was just severe angina.

HELEN: And milked for every last ounce of drama, I'll bet.

SOPHIE: And you're definitely pregnant?

HELEN: Yes.

SOPHIE: How is Martin reacting?

HELEN: With unusual indifference, I'm afraid. Mind you, nothing much raises Martin out of his torpor, but there's normally a bit more reaction than this.

SOPHIE: I read somewhere that there's a male menopause which is supposed to happen when they realise that they're never going to achieve what they thought they were going to achieve.

HELEN: He had his at twenty-three.

SOPHIE: Are his parents showing any interest?

HELEN: No. It's all a bit depressing. How's Jim taking to his new son?

SOPHIE: Oh, he's wildly enthusiastic. He just hates me. He's furious that I haven't stopped working on my thesis and become a 'good' mother.

HELEN: Where's all this study going to get you in the end?

SOPHIE: It's going to get me a decent job.

HELEN: Don't you think that looking after your children is your most important job?

SOPHIE: No.

HELEN: Why are you so desperate to embark upon a career?

SOPHIE: Because I'm sick of being treated like a mental defective by Jim and all his big-shot academic friends. I'm just as intelligent as they are but none of them take you seriously until you've got a string of degrees after your name.

HELEN: If you ask me they're a lot of intellectual snobs. Martin says his firm has stopped hiring graduates because they're arrogant and lazy and they haven't got any common sense.

SOPHIE: Martin's a graduate.

HELEN: They're a different type these days.

SOPHIE: Are the neighbours still giving you trouble?

HELEN: Yes. It's worse than ever. The ones on the left have stopped burning those huge mountains of leaves since I called the fire brigade, but now they ring the RSPCA every time our dog's water dish is empty.

SOPHIE: What about the other side?

HELEN: I'm winning that one. They confiscated three of Tobias's footballs so I've started him on the trumpet. Are you still planning to go up and show Mama the baby?

SOPHIE: Yes. If you can mind my kids for a day or two.

HELEN: Sure, what's another half dozen?

SOPHIE: When I'm up there I'll see if I can persuade her to come down.

HELEN: I wish she would. For the first time in my life I'm beginning to feel really low.

SCENE THREE

The cottage garden. A beautiful sunny day in early spring. A Schubert concerto is playing softly in the background.

FREDDY *is barbecuing meat on his newly completed edifice, a large, misshapen eyesore. He has had a few glasses of flagon red and is waxing eloquent.* FRANCES *is staring out onto the lake and pretending to listen.* FRANK *is further away, reading medical books and casting an occasional baleful eye at* FREDDY *and the barbecue.*

FREDDY: It was the most terrifying moment of my life. There I was with a hundred demoralised Australians behind me—and I'll tell you what: the Australian soldier is a fighter to the last, but when he does get demoralised he really goes and does the job properly—and behind us in hot pursuit the whole of the Japanese Imperial Army. And there in front of me was this Pommy colonel saying: 'I'm frightfully sorry, old chap, but there's absolutely no room on board for any of you'. I just saw red. Without even thinking I whipped out my pistol, stuck it in his gut and said: 'There's a hundred men behind me who aren't going to get shot to pieces because of some bloody obscure regulation that's floating around in your skull, mate, so you can either step aside or I'll pull this trigger'. He stepped aside.

FRANCES: Goodness. Were there any repercussions?

FREDDY: Yeah, I went up on a charge, but I had a hundred mates who would've shot the colonel if anything had happened to me and they knew it. I should stop boring you with this sort of stuff. I never let you talk about yourself.

FRANCES: There's not all that much to tell. I've led a very boring life compared to yours.

FREDDY: Mine was pretty boring too. I've just got a knack for picking out the interesting bits.

> FRANK's *look indicates that he doesn't think much of* FREDDY's *supposed knack.*

What sort of background did you come from, Frances?

FRANCES: My parents owned a modest property in the Western District of Victoria.

FREDDY: And they sent you to a good school. I can tell.

FRANCES: A very boring school, I'm afraid. I used to climb out of windows at the week-end and go riding horses. I was finally expelled.

FREDDY: Is one of your brothers running the property now?

FRANCES: We lost it in the Depression.

FRANK: [*to* FRANCES] I've read all I can on this cholesterol business and the circum-stantial evidence seems pretty strong, so I'm cutting out all meat.

FREDDY: Nice time to tell me that. Just when I finish your barbecue. [*To* FRANCES] You think it turned out all right?

FRANCES: It's a very impressive structure, Freddy.

FREDDY: Yeah, it's not too bad.

FRANCES: Did you work strictly to your plan?
FREDDY: Funnily enough, no. I just sort of let myself go and it came straight out of my head.
FRANK: Frances and I feel it's got a strange, haunting aura about it, Freddy. There's something of the Aztec, or perhaps it's Druid; we're not quite sure, but whatever it is we think it has enormous potential as the focal point for a new religion.
FREDDY: Stop pulling m'leg.
FRANK: No, seriously. We could all make a fortune.
FRANCES: It's a wonderful structure, Freddy, and it was very kind of you to do it.
FRANK: It was, Freddy, and the meat smells so good I think I'll wait till tomorrow to get onto my new regime. [*To* FRANCES] Apparently you can eat very well without meat with a little forethought and preparation. I'll get you a vegetarian cooking manual. Oh, and this theory that large doses of Vitamin E are beneficial seems worth a try. I'll put that on your shopping list for tomorrow, and in the afternoon, if you don't mind, you could drive me over to Saul's. My experiments with the various drugs are starting to come up with some answers. How long will the meat take, Freddy?
FREDDY: Five minutes or so.
FRANK: Good. I'll just go for a little stroll. Contrary to Saul's advice, there's a growing body of evidence that suggests that exercise, not rest, is the best thing for an ailing heart.
He walks offstage. FRANCES *and* FREDDY *watch him go.*
FREDDY: He takes his illness pretty seriously, doesn't he?
FRANCES: Yes, he does.
FREDDY: Look, er, Frances. If anything does happen to Frank, and I sincerely hope it doesn't, I just want you to know that you have someone around here who you can turn to.
FRANCES: Oh, er, thank you, Freddy. That's very sweet of you.
FREDDY: I've got this great big house up there on the hill and no one in it but me.

SCENE FOUR

Saul's surgery.

FRANK *reads a report to* SAUL *from a folder.* SAUL *is looking at the ceiling and fiddling with a ballpoint pen.*

FRANK: And the interesting thing is that I'm getting the same results after the attack as I was before. For instance, when I tried Aprinox for a month and switched to Lanoxin to Isordil—

SAUL: Perhaps we could have your conclusions.

FRANK: The conclusions are simply that the angina pain is less frequent and less intense when I take three Lanoxin daily and when I use Anginine for immediate relief.

SAUL: That's exactly what I prescribed for you in the very beginning.

FRANK: Yes, but you were just guessing. I've confirmed it all scientifically.

SAUL: Well, I'm glad it's all over. I've taken so many samples for you lately that the reps think I'm running a health racket.

FRANK: There is one problem with the Lanoxin that you didn't tell me about.

SAUL: What?

FRANK: Its side effects. It's got a tendency to cause agranulocytosis, which in simple terms is a lack of white blood cells—

SAUL: In simple terms?

FRANK: Sorry, I keep forgetting who's the doctor.

SAUL: So do I.

FRANK: I do think you should have warned me. I could be left without my first line of defence against trivial infection.

SAUL: It would be a reckless germ who tangled with you, Frank, but if you're worried I'll give you a blood test.

FRANK: I think you should.

SAUL: But not today. I have patients waiting.

FRANK: Saul. There is one other thing.

SAUL: What?

FRANK: I've always thought that a persistently morbid outlook on life is a sign of character weakness, but I'm afraid that lately I've been feeling a little depressed.

SAUL: My dear Frank. You have a serious heart condition, your hearing is getting worse, you are starting to have trouble with your vision… You'd be a mental oddity if you weren't a little depressed. You've got a lot of life left. Live it for its good moments.

FRANK: Frances' daughters are trying to take her away from me.

SAUL: Nonsense.

FRANK: I've got nothing to offer Frances anymore, Saul. I'm a sick old man and I'm going to get sicker, but I love her and depend on her and she loves me…

SAUL: Of course she does. It's obvious.

FRANK: But those two daughters of hers are luring her down south with an endless succession of babies.

SAUL: I'm sure that's not the only reason they're having them.

FRANK: Maybe not, but you put a squawking brat in front of a grandmother and her head goes soft, and those two down there know it.

SAUL: She's not going to leave you, Frank. I'd put money on it.

FRANK: I haven't told you the whole truth, Saul. There's another reason I'm depressed.

SAUL: What's that?

FRANK: I can't manage to do something I've always managed to do and it's giving me a bloody inferiority complex. I'd like you to prescribe a stimulant.

SAUL: A stimulant?

FRANK: Yes.

SAUL: Frank, you are nearly seventy-six, you have a weak heart, you have, I suspect, had more than your fair share of erotic satisfaction in life, so for heaven's sake grow old gracefully.

FRANK: I take it that means you won't.

SAUL: Certainly not. It'd kill you.

FRANK: Then give me some Tryptanol for my depression.

SAUL: [*reaching wearily for his prescription pad*] How do you spell it, Y or I?

SCENE FIVE

The cottage garden. A sunlit day.

FRANCES *leans over Sophie's carry cot and looks at the baby.* FRANK *listens to Mozart in the cottage.*

SOPHIE: Everyone says he looks like Jim.

FRANCES: He doesn't look like anyone. You were very brave bringing him all the way up here.

SOPHIE: I didn't think there was any other way you were going to see him. How is Frank's health now?

FRANCES: He's quite well, really.

SOPHIE: Why do you have to drive that big campervan around everywhere.

FRANCES: He's not supposed to do anything strenuous, and apart from that, the vision in his right eye has started to go.

SOPHIE: His eye?

FRANCES: And his hearing's deteriorating too.

SOPHIE: Is that why the music is so loud?

FRANCES *nods.*

So what does he do? Listen to music all day?

FRANCES: Sometimes he just thinks. Occasionally he even talks to me.

SOPHIE: What does he think about?

FRANCES: His past life. Apparently he's trying to make sense of it.

SOPHIE: How nice for him. Can he look after himself yet?

FRANCES: Yes. He's quite capable.

SOPHIE: So you will be able to come down and see Helen before the baby.

FRANCES: Yes. I've made up my mind.

SOPHIE: That's good. Helen's been quite depressed lately.

FRANCES: Why is she depressed?

SOPHIE: Apparently Martin and his parents are taking no interest in her pregnancy or in her.

FRANCES: I can't stand Martin's parents, I'm afraid.

SOPHIE: I can't stand Martin.

FRANCES: My mother would have called them the vulgar nouveau riche.

SOPHIE: Your mother would have been right.

FRANCES: I often wonder why she ever married into them.

SOPHIE: She wanted a husband, a home and security.

FRANCES: I don't suppose I can blame her. You both grew up through all those dreadful years of penny pinching.

SOPHIE: They were quite exciting years in a way.

FRANCES: I'm afraid they were very grim. It would have been easier to have stayed with your father. but after six years of marriage I just had no respect for his intelligence or integrity, and it's awful to live with someone you basically despise.

SOPHIE: Stop agonising, Mother.

FRANCES: You should have gone on to university. Your teachers all told me you should, but I would have had to borrow from your uncle and he'd just had Helen for four years—

SOPHIE: Stop agonising. I got there eventually.

FRANCES: You're kind to say those years were exciting.

SOPHIE: They were. We were always going on walks and hikes and trips on the train...

FRANCES: I could never stand sitting around in the one place for too long.

SOPHIE: One day you even took us off to a bushfire.

FRANCES: [*smiling*] I couldn't have been that silly, surely...

SOPHIE: You did. I can still remember the smell of the smoke and eucalyptus and I can remember men with black faces beating out the flames with wet bags.

FRANCES: Yes, you're right. I volunteered to go and make the men black tea. I must have been totally stupid. What if the wind had changed?

SOPHIE: I used to love those adventures.

FRANCES: Yes, you did, but Helen always wanted to go home. She liked order and stability and everything in its place.

SOPHIE: She'll be very glad to see you. I've never seen her quite so low.

SCENE SIX

Saul's surgery.

SAUL *sits at his desk. There is a knock at the door.* FRANCES *enters.*

FRANCES: Sorry I'm late. Are you sure I'm not taking up your time?

SAUL: It's more than a pleasure.

FRANCES: I just wanted to talk to you about Frank.

SAUL: Sit down.

FRANCES: Thank you. He wants to come with me to Melbourne. He said that you told him it would be perfectly all right.

SAUL: I told him that it would be most unwise.

FRANCES: It's terrible to say this, but I'm afraid I just don't want him to come.

SAUL: It's not a terrible thing to say. A man in his condition can be very
    demanding. You need a rest.

FRANCES: Yes I do.

SAUL: Then tell him straight out you don't want him to go.

FRANCES: He'll transform himself into a wounded martyr and I'll
    spend all my time down there feeling guilty. He's certain that my
    daughters are trying to lure me away from him.

SAUL: Are they?

FRANCES: Of course not. Do you think he definitely shouldn't go?

SAUL: It's one of those awkward situations where I can't give any
    definite advice. I'm sure the journey and climate will be bad for
    him if he goes but if he stays behind he'll worry, and worry isn't
    good for him either.

FRANCES: Mmm.

SAUL: I'm afraid it's your decision. One thing before you go, Frances,
    and this is a little embarrassing. I, er, don't think you should expect
    too much of him these days.

FRANCES: I don't. I do everything for him.

SAUL: I, er, was talking about the, er, private areas. Which again is the
    wrong choice of words. What I am trying to say, and saying it very
    badly, is that I think it's unwise to think of him engaging in intimate
    activity in his present condition.

FRANCES: Of course.

SAUL: He asked me to prescribe him a stimulant.

FRANCES: Not at my bidding, I can assure you.

SAUL: I tried to tell him that in the twilight years one should be
    content to reflect on past glories, but he wasn't impressed. [*Pause.*]
    Frances, if anything does happen to him, and I sincerely hope it
    doesn't, I'd just like you to know that there is someone around
    here who would do anything he could to help you for as long as
    you'd like to be helped.

FRANCES: I'm, er, very touched, Saul. Thank you.

SCENE SEVEN

Melbourne.

FRANK *strides up and down Helen's living room with a big rug wrapped around him. He now wears a hearing aid. The radio is playing Beethoven very loudly, and* FRANK *conducts as he strides.* HELEN, *heavily pregnant, enters with* JOAN.

HELEN: Here he is, if you can get him to notice you.

JOAN: Excuse me, maestro.

FRANK: Joan! Wonderful to see you.

JOAN: Hope I'm not interrupting?

FRANK: No, it's just Malcolm Sargent making a mess of Beethoven as usual. How are you, my dear? You're looking well.

JOAN: So are you.

HELEN: [*with a forced smile*] I'd appreciate it if you could keep the volume down just a little, Frank. You've woken Janessa.

FRANK: Hmm. [*Going to turn it down, muttering*] A bit of Beethoven won't do her any harm.

HELEN: Are you cold, Frank?

FRANK: No. I'm pretending to be an Indian.

HELEN: Turn on the heater, for heaven's sake.

FRANK: I'm fine.

HELEN: Well, it's your own fault if you don't.

HELEN *leaves.*

JOAN: It really is cold, Dad. Turn on the heater.

FRANK: If I do, the subject of fuel bills will wend its way into the dinner table conversation tonight with all the delicacy of a draught horse's fart.

JOAN: Like that, is it?

FRANK: Like that? It's a thousand times worse. That woman has done a five-year course in how to make guests uncomfortable and graduated with first-class honours. I'm still under heavy suspicion of having damaged a geranium during my morning stroll.

JOAN: You should make allowances for the fact she's pregnant, Dad. When's she due?

FRANK: Two weeks ago. At this rate, the bloody thing'll be three years old before it's born. Frances is being worked like a slave. She's just an unpaid domestic servant. At any rate, enough of my problems. How are you?

JOAN: Fine.

FRANK: Eric is too busy to come across and see me, I presume?

JOAN: That's what he says.

FRANK: Why does he hate me so much?

JOAN: Mum said you were at each other's throats almost from the minute he was born. It was a case of two dominant personalities meeting head-on.

FRANK: I did everything a good father is supposed to do—took him fishing every school holidays...

JOAN: He hated fishing.

FRANK: Well, that's his problem, the snotty little twerp. Is he still president of his local Liberal Party branch?

JOAN: I think so.

FRANK: He became a conservative just to spite me. It's a terrible thing to think that my genes are being handed down to future generations via a right-wing real estate swindler.

JOAN: Come on, Dad. He's not as bad as that.

FRANK: I hope you're going to have children some day and redress the balance.

JOAN: I'm a little bit hesitant to become a wife and mother right at the moment.

FRANK: Don't get too obsessed with this new wave of feminism, Joan. Socialism is the only important path to the future. Feminism is just a sidetrack.

JOAN: [*smiling*] Having known some of the men intent on leading us to the Socialist future, I think I'll stick to the sidetrack.

FRANK: Hmm. I'm Spending an increasing amount of my time these days reviewing my past life, Joan—trying to make sense of it all. I've thoroughly gone into my relationship with Eric and come to the conclusion that his deficiencies are his own fault. I'm not to blame. But certain things you said at our last meeting about the way I'm supposed to have treated your mother puzzled me. I did, I admit, become embroiled in certain romantic dalliances which caused your mother pain and were probably unwise, but there were extenuating circumstances which you probably don't know about—

JOAN: I wasn't referring to—

FRANK: Let me finish. I want to explain something to you so that you don't judge me too harshly. I married your mother at twenty-two when she was only nineteen, and we were both very much in love, but unfortunately we were both almost totally naive, so that when I grabbed her passionately and, I must admit, clumsily, on our wedding night, she was so shocked that she turned to me and said, 'Don't ever do that again,' and unfortunately she meant it. Now it wasn't my fault and it wasn't hers, it was due to the general ignorance of the times—

JOAN: Dad, I really wasn't referring to your romantic dalliances.

FRANK: What were you referring to?

JOAN: Let's talk about something else.

FRANK: No, please. I must know what you're referring to.

JOAN: You assumed that the whole purpose of her life was to wait on you hand and foot. You scarcely ever spoke to her except to issue commands, and you had no respect for her sensitivity and intelligence.

FRANK: That's not true.

JOAN: Let's change the subject.

FRANK: Give me one example of when I ever treated your mother with less than total respect.

JOAN: There were so many, Dad.

FRANK: One. Give me one!

JOAN: If you must have an example the one that springs most vividly to mind is the time when you and Eric were arguing politics over one of Mum's excellent but rarely noticed meals, and she offered one of her rare opinions—a quite reasonable opinion if I remember correctly—and you turned to her and said, 'Stick to your cooking, Eve, you haven't got the brains of a gnat'.

FRANK: [*stunned*] I would never have said that.

JOAN: Maybe it wasn't quite as blunt.

FRANK: I would never have said that. If I did it's unforgivable.

JOAN: I'm sorry, Dad. I shouldn't have mentioned it.

Pause. JOAN *looks away.*

FRANK: One thing I'll have to face about myself, I suppose, is that while I've always loved mankind in general, I have been less than generous to some of those I've been involved with in particular. Didn't Eric send any message at all?

JOAN: Yes. He said that if Whitlam ever gets into office, the private sector of our economy is going to be irreparably damaged.

FRANK: Well, you just tell him that Whitlam is a man of enormous political and intellectual stature, who, despite the basic conservatism of his political stance, makes our more recent Prime Ministers look like parliamentary pygmies. What a line-up. Flippers Holt, Shagger Gorton and Twinkle-Toes McMahon. And God help us if we ever get Snedden. Tell him I had a collie dog who had more brains than Snedden!

SCENE EIGHT

Melbourne.

FRANCES *talks with* SOPHIE *and* HELEN. HELEN *is no longer pregnant.*

FRANCES: She's a lovely baby, Helen.

HELEN: Do you like her name?

FRANCES: Most distinctive. I shouldn't drink any more. I'm getting quite drunk.

SOPHIE: Why not get drunk? It's a rare occasion that we're all together. Here's to Oriana.

ALL: [*toasting the name*] Oriana.

HELEN: Are you sure you like that name?

FRANCES: Is it too late to change it?

HELEN: No. I just thought of it today.

FRANCES: Well, it does have a familiar ring. Isn't it an ocean liner?

HELEN: Oh, migod. So it is. We can't have that.

FRANCES: How about something simple? You've both got so many exotic names that a family gathering is getting to sound a bit florid. Call her Jill.

HELEN: Jill? Jill? Yes, why not?

ALL: [*toasting the name*] Jill.

HELEN: Mother, don't go back up north straight away.

SOPHIE: Come and stay with us for a while.

FRANCES: Frank's very keen to get moving again and he really isn't very well.

HELEN: Stay a bit longer, Mama. You're just starting to enjoy yourself.

FRANCES: Yes, I am. Thank you for that wonderful night out, Sophie.

HELEN: Did you enjoy the play?

FRANCES: Yes. Sophie, you really shouldn't have taken me to that grand restaurant. It must have cost Jim a fortune.

SOPHIE: He can afford it now that he's a professor.

FRANCES: You must be glad that you've nearly finished your thesis. Are you going to try and find a job?

SOPHIE: I've been offered some part-time tutoring but I don't think I'll take it.

FRANCES: Why not?

SOPHIE: It all seems so futile. I have to start at the very bottom rung and Jim's a bloody professor.

FRANCES: You've got to start somewhere.

SOPHIE: I just don't know whether I've got the energy.

FRANCES: That doesn't sound like you, Sophie.

SOPHIE: What am I supposed to sound like?

FRANCES: When you were a child you were always so positive and adventurous. You mustn't let yourself become morose.

SOPHIE: I'm sorry we had that argument in front of you last night, Mama, but Jim just wants me to shut up and let him get on with his career.

FRANCES: Do you both want a word of advice? I'd normally never try and give any, but I'm drunk and rather worried. I think you should take that job, Sophie, even if it's nothing much to start with, because if you don't you're going to end up one of those bitter, unpleasant wives who drink too much.

SOPHIE: That's not fair, Mama. I don't usually drink as much as I did last night.

FRANCES: I should hope not.

SOPHIE: Was I very embarrassing?

FRANCES: Well, I don't think Jim appreciated it when you stood up and told the restaurant that if they formed an orderly queue he'd autograph their menus. I think you should take that job.

SOPHIE: I know, but I just can't stand the thought of starting at the very, very bottom.

HELEN: In my opinion you should just concentrate on being a good mother.

FRANCES: Different people need to do different things, Helen. [*To*

SOPHIE] I used to watch you running down the hill to the beach with your hair streaming behind you and I used to think that you were the very epitome of freedom and exuberance and zest.

SOPHIE: And now I've lost it all. Is that what you're saying?

FRANCES: I just hate to see that bitterness and sense of defeat creeping in. I know that if you had gone on with your studies and become qualified when you were younger then you might have had an established career by now, so I blame myself for a lot of what's happened, but if you take that job you've still got a chance.

SOPHIE: Yes, you're right. There's no sense whining. If that's what I want, I've got to start at the bottom and battle my way up.

HELEN: It's obvious why I was never the favourite. I didn't spend enough of my youth running down hills with my hair streaming behind me.

SOPHIE: Shut up, Helen. You're paranoid.

HELEN: Well, tell me one thing I did when I was young, Mama. I bet you can't even remember.

FRANCES: You used to sit on the beach making sandhouses for soldier crabs and give them a tongue-lashing if they didn't behave.

SOPHIE: So what's changed?

HELEN: Shut up.

FRANCES: The positive thing about you, Helen, was that you always said what you thought and never let yourself be bullied. I suppose that's why I find it difficult to understand why you worry so much about what Martin's parents think.

HELEN: Is this my bit of advice coming up?

FRANCES: Yes, it is. I know we were poor and they were rich, and I know they think their son married beneath him, and I know they disapprove of the fact that Frank and I aren't married, but for heaven's sake, who cares?

HELEN: I don't.

SOPHIE: You do.

FRANCES: Yesterday when you should have been resting, you cleaned every square inch of the house on the off-chance they might arrive.

HELEN: All right. They do put the fear of God into me, but you've never seen them in action. Old Roma prowls through the house hunting dirt and grime like a tax lawyer after a loophole.

SOPHIE: Why do you put up with it? They're monsters.

HELEN: I know, but I've got to live with them.

FRANCES: Of course you have, my dear, but don't let them walk all over you.

SOPHIE: I'll drink to that!

HELEN: Do you really have to go, Mama?

FRANCES: I'm afraid so.

SOPHIE: Are you sure he's sick?

FRANCES: He's full of aches and pains.

HELEN: What's this Sophie tells me about you rowing him around the lake?

FRANCES: Yes, the old boy can be pretty demanding when the fish are biting. He sits up in the stern scanning the lake like Captain Ahab, and all of a sudden he'll shout, 'Head for the broken water near Mosses Point,' and no sooner do we get there then he'll yell, 'The buggers are gone. Head for the estuary.' It can be a bit tiring on the arms.

HELEN: The rotten old despot.

FRANCES: Well, it would be a little better if he'd talk to me sometimes, but I'm afraid he just sits there with his jaw slack looking quite imbecilic. Apparently he's thinking.

SOPHIE: You shouldn't feel you have to go up there with him again if you don't want to, Mama.

FRANCES: I'm not really looking forward to it. There are so many things starting to go wrong with him.

HELEN: Like that old Vauxhall we used to have.

SOPHIE: We could never work out how it kept going.

FRANCES: It's a bit the same with Frank.

SCENE NINE

A hospital, Melbourne.

FRANK *is in a hospital bed. Tubes drip into him and wires connect him to an oscilloscope.* FRANK *watches the blips on the oscilloscope narrowly.* FRANCES *enters.*

FRANCES: Hello, dear. How are you today?

FRANK: Terrible.

FRANCES: Have they got the results of the tests?

FRANK: Yes. It was a major heart attack. I knew that Melbourne would damn near finish me.

FRANCES: But you're going to be all right now?

FRANK: If I last through the next ten days there's a good chance I'll survive.

FRANCES: You're starting to get a little colour back in your cheeks.

FRANK: They must be putting vegetable dye in the drip, because there's no damn blood flowing. See that weak little blip there? That's my heart.

FRANCES: How long do they think you'll be in here?

FRANK: Three weeks. As soon as I get up we're heading up north.

FRANCES: Will they let you travel?

FRANK: I don't give a bugger whether they will or not. I'm going.

FRANCES: It mightn't be a good idea

FRANK: If you won't take me I'll go by train.

FRANCES: Of course I'll take you, but—

FRANK: I suppose Goneril and Regan have been urging you to stay down here?

FRANCES: Fran —

FRANK: Taking you out to shows and filling you with champagne. It won't last long, you know. As soon as I've gone they'll have you down on your knees scrubbing the floors again.

FRANCES: Frank, how many times do I have to tell you? I love you and I'm staying with you until—

FRANK: Until I croak, which mightn't be all that long. My blips are erratic today. Thanks, my dear. I do appreciate your loyalty. I can't offer you champagne every night, but there'll be a magnum when I die.

FRANCES: It's a magnum I'm not really looking forward to.

FRANK: Me neither.

FRANCES: You must be very bored in here.

FRANK: I am. All I can do is sit here watching my own heartbeat on the oscilloscope. It does have the odd exciting moment, though. A circuit blew out the other day and my blip stopped. I thought I'd died.

SCENE TEN

Melbourne.

FRANCES, HELEN *and* SOPHIE *discuss Frank's attack.*

HELEN: There's no question about it, Mama. You're not going up there again now.

SOPHIE: He'll get much better care down here.

FRANCES: He's terrified that if he doesn't go back up north he'll die.

HELEN: Well, he's just being stupid and infantile. I think it's outrageous that he expects you to drive him all the way back up there in that damn campervan.

FRANCES: I drove it all the way down.

SOPHIE: Mama, the important thing is, do you want to go?

FRANCES: No, of course I don't want to go.

HELEN: Then don't.

FRANCES: Helen, it's not as simple as that. He's really got it fixed in his mind that he won't last more than a few weeks if he stays down here.

HELEN: You're not responsible for the fact that he has totally irrational beliefs.

FRANCES: They're not totally irrational. The cold does thicken the blood.

HELEN: He can sit inside in front of the heater.

FRANCES: It's just not physical, it's psychological. He wants the colours and the light. He really is terrified that if he stays down here much longer he's going to die. I'm the only person that can take him up there and care for him, and if I don't I've got to live with the knowledge that he's sitting down here depressed and miserable and scared.

SOPHIE: Mother, he's not your responsibility.

FRANCES: He is my responsibility. You were both right. I went into this relationship impulsively, I didn't think ahead—and all the things you predicted have come true, so now I've got to live with it.

HELEN: What about your responsibility to us? We do like to see you now and then.

FRANCES: I'll do my best to come down as often as possible.

HELEN: Frank isn't the only one who could use some help. I've been as depressed as hell ever since you left. I'm getting no support or affection from Martin or his parents and I just can't cope and now I've had the baby it's going to be ten times worse.

FRANCES: I know it is, dear. and I wish I could be here to help, but I have to go up north with Frank.

HELEN: I see. Dumped when I was eight and dumped again now.

SOPHIE: Helen, sometimes you don't know when to shut up.

HELEN: Well, that's how I feel.

FRANCES: What exactly do you want me to do, Helen?

HELEN: Come and live in your room again.

FRANCES: What about Frank?

HELEN: Let his daughter look after him. For God's sake, Mama, where do your priorities lie—with someone you've known two and a half years or with your own daughter?

FRANCES: Helen, you can't use that sort of logic.

SOPHIE: Don't be such a selfish little bitch.

HELEN: Go on. Gang up on me. The both of you. As always.

SOPHIE: No one's ganging up on you.

FRANCES: Ganging up on you!

HELEN: I've never been given a fair go all my life and when I finally ask for a little bit of help I'm called a selfish bitch.

SOPHIE: Well, you are.

HELEN: And you're a bloody bully. I haven't forgotten all those ghost stories at night to scare me out of my wits and I remember how you used to put me in the old pram and push me down the hill and roar with laughter every time I fell out.

SOPHIE: You got what you deserved. You were a pain in the arse.

FRANCES: Stop it! You were both pains in the arse. You took after your father.

SOPHIE: Well, she's got no right to say things like that about you.

FRANCES: Yes she has. I should never have left her and I've always known it, and that's exactly why I can't run out on Frank now. I took on this responsibility with my eyes open and I must see it through.

SCENE ELEVEN

The cottage. Light and brightness. Sunshine.

A new, bright red phone sits on the coffee table. It rings several times.

FRANCES *staggers into the kitchen carrying a carton full of groceries. She puts down her shopping and races to the phone. When she answers it her voice is weary and a little distracted.*

FRANCES: Oh, Saul. Yes. Just a minute till I get a pen. Right. The twenty-second. Right. And that's the eye specialist or the ear specialist? Eye. Ear is on the twenty-fifth. Eye at eleven fifteen, ear at eleven forty-five. Eye at your surgery. Ear at Outpatients. The ambulance will come for ear, but I drive Frank across for eye. Right. And the next visit is on the twenty-seventh at two-thirty. Thanks, Saul.

She hangs up and sighs wearily before going to the groceries and starting to unpack them. FRANK *comes in the door of the cottage, leaning on a stick, with a patch over one eye and wearing a hearing aid. He is frail and moves gingerly; but rather than seeming at death's door, he exudes a certain bright-eyed energy that gives him the air of a geriatric pirate or a Victorian rake. He picks up an eggtimer.*

FRANK: If that was Melbourne you should've been using the eggtimer.

FRANCES: It wasn't.

FRANK: Who was it?

FRANCES: Saul. He was checking your specialists' appointments.

FRANK: Did you tell him that my eye is still aching?

FRANCES: No, I'm sorry. I forgot.

FRANK: Blast.

FRANCES: I'm sorry. I forgot.

FRANK: What did that obsequious, rednecked thug who runs the general store charge you for the cashews?

FRANCES: A dollar thirty-eight.

FRANK: That's the third price rise in three months.

FRANCES: He says there's a worldwide shortage.

FRANK: I bet. Some cunning cartel has cornered the world market. I'll warrant that none of the price rise is going into the pockets of the poor peasants picking the things out there in the South American jungles. Did they get in the bran and the brewer's yeast?

FRANCES: Yes.

FRANK: Did you get the vitamin E tablets?

FRANCES: Yes, they're there.

FRANK: The lentils and leeks?

FRANCES: Yes.

FRANK: The alfalfa and seaweed?

FRANCES: Yes, yes. I got everything.

FRANK: [*looking at his watch*] It's time for my Promite.

FRANCES: I've just put the kettle on.

FRANK: I've been reading this diet book and it appears that it's much better to shred the carrots. You release about seventeen percent more of the vitamins that way. My dear, are you listening?

> FRANCES *is obviously eager to read her letters. She stops opening them and looks up.*

FRANCES: Yes, dear, I am.

FRANK: Are there any for me?

FRANCES: Not today.

FRANK: I suppose they're from the baby farm down south?

FRANCES: Yes. There's one from Sophie and one from Helen. Sophie's put some photos in. Look at young Tarquin. He'll be five in a week. Can you believe that? Five.

FRANK: Five.

FRANCES: It's incredible isn't it?

FRANK: It's shattering. In the face of a catastrophic South-East Asian war and impending Federal elections, it is nonetheless shattering.

FRANCES: He knows the alphabet.

FRANK: Another two weeks and he'll be reading Shakespeare. Tarquin! Do those idiots down there know who Tarquin was?

FRANCES: He's drawn a picture of a cat at the bottom of the letter.

FRANK: A Roman despot who had the unfortunate habit of raping anything that moved.

FRANCES: Would you prefer me to read the letters outside?

FRANK: Sorry. [*Pause.*] I can't find my spanners.

FRANCES: Spanners?

FRANK: Did you lend them to Freddy?

FRANCES: I don't know.

FRANK: Well, did you or didn't you?

FRANCES: What do they look like?

FRANK: Spanners? The things that tighten nuts! A handle with a bulge at both ends!

FRANCES: I lent them to Freddy.

FRANK: Well, don't lend them to Freddy.

FREDDY *knocks at the door and comes in.*

FREDDY: Did I hear my name being used in vain?

FRANK: Have you got my spanners?

FREDDY: Don't worry. You'll get 'em back.

FRANK: Well, I need them now. I've got hairs in the carburettor again.

FREDDY: [*to* FRANCES] Do you want me to bring it in?

FRANCES: He doesn't deserve it, but you may as well.

FREDDY *goes outside and comes in carrying a huge, high-backed reclining chair.*

FRANK: My God. What's that?

FRANCES: A present.

FRANK: From who?

FRANCES: From me. For your birthday. It's specially designed to give maximum support and relaxation.

FRANK: It looks hideous.

FREDDY: Come on, Frank. Don't look a gift horse in the mouth. Happy seventy-seventh.

FRANK: Where did you get the money?

FRANCES: I saved.

FREDDY: Sit down and I'll show you how it works.

FRANK: What do you mean, 'how it works'? Has it got a four-cylinder engine inside it or something.

FREDDY: Sit down.

FRANK *sits down reluctantly.* FREDDY *pulls the back and* FRANK *jerks back into a half-supine position.*

Comfortable?

FRANK: Is it real leather?

FRANCES: I'm afraid not, but I can cover it with a nice fabric.

FREDDY: Pull that lever.

FRANK *looks at him suspiciously, but pulls the lever at the side of the chair. A foot support shoots out on an expander mechanism.*

FRANK: Hmm.

He pulls the lever again and the footrest shoots back into the chair.

Hmm. That's quite clever.

He pulls the lever several times, fascinated with it. He reclines and operates the footrest again.

Quite comfortable too.

FRANCES *moves across with* FRANK'*s mug of Promite.*

FRANCES: Two heaped teaspoons, my dear?

FRANK *nods.*

FRANK: Otherwise it tastes like creek water downstream from a dead cow.

FREDDY: I've got my own little present wrapped in brown bottles up the hill. I'll be right back.

FRANK: Thanks, Freddy.

FREDDY *leaves.* FRANK *operates the chair.* FRANCES *comes across carrying an iced cake with candles on it.*

A cake.

FRANCES: Yes, and don't complain. It's wholemeal with no eggs.

She opens the other letter and starts reading.

FRANK: I'll be able to listen to my concerts in comfort.

FRANCES: [*reading*] Yes, you will.

FRANK: Who's that one from?

FRANCES: Helen.

FRANK: How are things?

FRANCES: Martin is having an affair with another woman.

FRANK: I'm surprised. I would have thought that passion for anything but his sales charts was beyond him.

FRANCES: It's apparently serious. He's shifting out.

FRANK: Who can blame him? Twelve years of that tongue would be enough for anyone.

FRANCES: [*angrily*] She's my daughter and I love her, and from the sound of the letter she's utterly miserable.

Pause.

FRANK: I suppose you'll be going down there.

FRANCES: Yes, I will.

FRANK: How long will you be gone?

FRANCES: Possibly for good.

FRANK: For good? Why?

FRANCES: Why? Because you're a rude, arrogant, despotic old bully and I can't stand living with you a minute longer! And just for your information, Helen has been sending me money for years. It's the only reason we've been able to exist!

FRANCES *storms into a side room in a fury, leaving* FRANK *looking surprised and worried.*

SCENE TWELVE

The cottage. Night.

FRANK *is in bed propped up with pillows.* FREDDY *lies on the floor nearby in a sleeping bag.*

FRANK: It's good of you to come down again, Freddy. I appreciate it.

FREDDY: No worries.

FRANK: Normally I wouldn't bother you, but I'm starting to get persistent pains in the back and that is not a very good sign, and if anything did happen it's comforting to think that there's someone here who could get on the phone.

FREDDY: No worries. My wife said I used to snore.

FRANK: She was right. You were in fine voice last night.

FREDDY: Sorry about that.

FRANK: Not at all. In the circumstances it's a very welcome sound indeed.

FREDDY: Still haven't heard from Frances?

FRANK: No.

FREDDY: Why don't you phone her?

FRANK: No.

FREDDY: Or send a letter.

FRANK: I won't beg. I've never done it in my life and I won't start now.

FREDDY: I think you should swallow your pride and admit you were in the wrong.

FRANK: Hmm. Easier said than done. [*Pause.*] Who are you going to vote for?

FREDDY: Whitlam.

FRANK: That's quite a turnabout.

FREDDY: Yeah. I still don't like unions, mind you. The one I was a member of made us vote with a show of hands and if we didn't vote the right way we got bashed up later.

FRANK: So why are you changing your vote?

FREDDY: I've changed my mind about Vietnam.

FRANK: Good for you.

FREDDY: I couldn't cop some of those photos of the napalm victims.

FRANK: We're in for a new era, Freddy.

FREDDY: Were you really a Communist once?

FRANK: Yes, for thirty years. There was a wonderful period after the War when Fascism had been defeated and we thought a new order of justice and fraternity was going to sweep the world. It didn't turn out to be that simple.

FREDDY: I think Whitlam's going to toss McMahon.

FRANK: He is. We're in for a new era. Unfortunately, I don't think I'll be around to see very much of it.

FREDDY: Come on, mate. That's no way to talk. Do you want me to get you a mug of Promite?

FRANK: Frankly, I can't think of anything I'd like less.

FREDDY: I could stiffen it up a bit, but I don't suppose Saul would approve.

FRANK: Bugger Saul.

FREDDY: One rum and Promite coming up.

FRANK: Go easy on the Promite.

SCENE THIRTEEN

Melbourne.

FRANCES *sits with a tearful* HELEN.

FRANCES: Where are they living?

HELEN: In a flat in South Yarra. I wouldn't mind so much if there was some substance to her but she's a total non-event. She's a mealy-mouthed, washed-out, pouting, simpering, gormless, vapid, stupid little creature without a mind of her own or a thought in her head. For him to run off with someone like that is just an incredible insult.

FRANCES: Does he want to see the children?

HELEN: He may very well want to, but there is no way, no way that he's going to get anywhere near them while he's living with that loathsome woman. He's gone insane, Mama. Apart from everything else she's overweight, asthmatic and has dermatitis. It's just such an insult, Mama. A calculated insult. I've been to my lawyer, and he's going to be very, very sorry.

FRANCES: How have Martin's parents reacted?

HELEN: They've been really wonderful. They've totally disowned him. Roma is round here every day looking after the children and Reg is keeping the garden in shape.

FRANCES: Really?

HELEN: They've been wonderful. They just can't understand how any son of theirs could do that to his children.

FRANCES: Has Sophie been helping out?

HELEN: Sophie? I've hardly seen her.

FRANCES: Why didn't she take the job she was offered?

HELEN: It wasn't good enough for her. She and Jim are just having one blazing row after another these days and I'm afraid I just don't want to know about it in the circumstances. I'll just go and check the mail. My lawyer says Martin hasn't got a leg to stand on. He's going to lose the house, the car—the lot!

She leaves. FRANCES *sits there looking a little depressed.*

SCENE FOURTEEN

Evening.

FRANCES *sits by the phone in Melbourne.* FRANK *sits by the phone in the cottage. The phone rings beside* FRANCES. *She picks it up.*

OPERATOR: [*voice-over*] 233 4509? Mrs Frances Oldfield?

FRANCES: That's right.

OPERATOR: [*voice-over*] Hold the line, please. Boolindawhy calling.

The phone beside FRANK *rings. He picks it up.*

Boolindawhy. I have your Melbourne number. Go ahead.

FRANK: Hmm. Frances?

FRANCES: Frank?

FRANK: Yes. Hmm. How are you?

FRANCES: I'm well. And you?

FRANK: Could be worse. Hmm. I've been thinking back over my past life, Frances, and I've realised that while I've been in love with mankind in general I've been very thoughtless to some of those I've been involved with in particular... Are you there?

FRANCES: Yes. I'm here.

FRANK: So I've rung up to apologise. Hmm. Needless to say I'm missing you very much and if you ever did see fit to return you can rest assured I'd never treat you as badly again. I'd also be willing to contemplate marriage... Are you still there?

FRANCES: Yes, I'm here.

FRANK: I'm, er, hmm, sincere about what I say, Frances, so please think it over because I really do, hmm, love you... Are you there?

FRANCES: Yes, I'm here.

FRANK: Well, I won't keep you. Saul and Freddy send their love. [*Pause.*] Well, I won't keep you. Goodbye for now.

FRANCES: Goodbye.

They hang up their respective phones.

SCENE FIFTEEN

The cottage interior. Day.

FRANK *sits in his chair listening to Bach on the radio. It is the Brandenburg Concerto Number Five, second movement.* FRANCES *enters.* FREDDY *follows carrying a suitcase. He puts the suitcase down, grins awkwardly at* FRANK, *and leaves.* FRANK *gets up out of his chair They stare at each other, then embrace.*

FRANK: Your description of me as a bully and a despot was hard but fair. I'll be a different man from now on. And I was totally sincere about the marriage.

FRANCES: I didn't come back because of that.

FRANK: Perhaps not, but I meant it. Not in a church. I couldn't go as far as that, but we'll do everything else.

FRANCES: Marriage doesn't mean anything to you, Frank.

FRANK: Yes it does. It means you'll think twice before you walk out on me the next time.

They hug.

Now please, will you marry me?

FRANCES: Yes. If you really want to.

FRANK: Good. We'll do it properly. A honeymoon in Sydney—the lot. Now sit down and I'll make you a cup of tea. [*Putting on the kettle*] I was very lonely without you.

FRANCES: And I was lonely without you.

FRANK: I thought that I'd lost you for good. I know how close you are to your daughters and how close they are to you and I'm touched and a little overwhelmed that you chose to come back.

FRANCES: Frank…

FRANK: No, I'm being serious. I've very little to offer anyone and I can't help feeling I don't really deserve you.

FRANCES: Frank. I don't want you to think I don't love you, but the truth of the matter is that I had nowhere else to go.

FRANK: What do you mean? Helen—

FRANCES: Helen and Sophie are working their own lives out. I can't do anything more for them now.

SCENE SIXTEEN

The cottage. Day.

SAUL *sits in a chair looking morose.*

SAUL: Frank, you must not go down to Sydney.

FRANK: [*offstage*] What's that?

SAUL: You must not—

FRANK: [*offstage*] I'm going.

SAUL: Reason with him, Frances.

FRANCES: [*offstage*] I've tried.

> FRANK *enters in his underclothes, black eye patch and his hearing aid, and proceeds to dress himself in an immaculate white suit.*

FRANK: We're going to be married and then we're going off to young Brett Whiteley's exhibition and nothing is going to stop us.

SAUL: Your heart is going to stop you.

FRANK: Do you want to bet?

SAUL: You know enough to know what those persistent back pains mean.

FRANK: Lumbago.

SAUL: Lumbago. It's your heart protesting. If you don't have a complete rest you'll kill yourself.

FRANK: Fiddle faddle. I'll bet ten dollars that I'll outlive you.

SAUL: Don't joke.

FRANK: I'm serious.

SAUL: I don't make bets about things like that. It's bad luck.

FRANK: Ten dollars.

SAUL: All right. Anything you say. Ten dollars, but will you give up this idea—?

FRANK: And when I get back I want something done about this hearing aid. It amplifies, but there's no clarity.

SAUL: Please, for the last time…

> FRANCES *appears wearing a simple but very pretty dress.*

Frances, tell him not to go.

FRANCES: I've tried.

FRANK: Look at that. The bridegroom in white and the bride in red. How times have changed.

> FREDDY *comes in the door carrying a camera and a flashbulb.*

FREDDY: Frances, you look fantastic. Can I kiss the bride?

FRANK: Not until we're married, and then only briefly.

FREDDY: They look great, don't they, Saul?

SAUL: Terrific.

FREDDY: Let's have you over here.

> *The camera clicks but the flashbulb does not go off.*

FRANK: We haven't got time for photographs.

FREDDY: Damn!

FRANK: Come on, man. The train goes in twenty minutes. Can't we take the picture outside?

FREDDY: No, I want one in the cottage. Out of the way, Saul. Let's try again.

FRANK: All right. What do we do? Say cheese? Smile, slouch, lounge or grin?

FREDDY: Just look relaxed.

FRANK: It's hard to when you know you've got nineteen minutes to catch the train.

The flash goes off.

FREDDY: Right.

FRANK: I hate photos. They never make me look intelligent enough.

FREDDY: [*to* FRANCES] What he lacks in youth he makes up for in modesty.

> FRANK, FRANCES *and* FREDDY *go out the door.* SAUL *shrugs and follows.*

FRANK: [*offstage*] Is my toothbrush packed, Frances?

FRANCES: [*offstage*] Yes, dear. Just get in the van.

SCENE SEVENTEEN

Sydney.

FRANK, *dressed in his smart white suit, stands next to* FRANCES *in front of a civil* WEDDING CELEBRANT *whose unctuous, patronising manner indicates that he thinks* FRANK *must be senile.*

CELEBRANT: Can I just say before we begin what a great privilege it is for me to be marrying a couple like yourselves.

FRANK: Why? What's so different about us?

CELEBRANT: I sometimes can't help thinking that the young people of today think that happiness is reserved for them and them alone.

FRANK: They're ninety-nine percent right.

CELEBRANT: [*ignoring this*] So I personally find it a wonderful thing when people in the autumn of their lives find love.

FRANK: Then let's get started, shall we, before autumn slips into winter.

CELEBRANT: Can I just say, Mr Brown, it is terribly heartening to find someone of your age with so much spirit.

FRANK: The spirit is willing but the flesh is damned weak, so could you stop your patronising chatter and just get on with it.

SCENE EIGHTEEN

A Sydney art gallery.

FRANK *and* FRANCES, *still in their wedding attire, approach a desk behind which sits a female* ATTENDANT. *They go to pass but she stops them.*

ATTENDANT: Excuse me, sir, madam. Do you have an invitation?

FRANK: Invitation? Why do we need an invitation?

ATTENDANT: This is a private preview, sir. The gallery is open to the general public tomorrow.

FRANK: This is preposterous. I'm Brett Whiteley's father. Go and get my boy immediately and we'll straighten this thing out.

ATTENDANT: Oh. I'm terribly sorry, Mr Whiteley. I should have recognised you.

FRANK: Ah, you can't be blamed. I don't often come to his openings. If you want my opinion he's far too obsessed with sex.

ATTENDANT: Well, this show is a little on the erotic side. I hope you're not upset.

FRANK: If we are we'll let him know about it. We didn't bring him up to be like that, did we, Maud?

FRANCES: No. I really don't know where he got it from. Could we have a catalogue, please?

ATTENDANT: Of course. Have two.

The ATTENDANT *watches them as they go inside.*

SCENE NINETEEN

The cottage garden. A beautiful sunlit day.

SAUL *sits on a bench.* FRANK *comes down to join him. He looks tired and frail, but buoyant.*

FRANK: Frances and I have added our votes to the tide that is going to sweep in a new era. Have you voted?

SAUL: I never vote. Did you enjoy Sydney?

FRANK: Wonderful. And just between you and me, something happened down there that I thought I'd never experience again.

SAUL: If you're talking about what I think you're talking about, it's a miracle you aren't dead.

FRANK: Maybe it was unwise. but we were in a motel room on our honeymoon and we'd just come from that damned Brett Whiteley exhibition. The combined impetus was overwhelming.

SAUL: Sit down.

FRANK: I can't. My concert starts in a few minutes. But don't go. Frances will be down in a minute.

He goes up the path. FRANCES *comes down with a mug of Promite.*

You shouldn't have, my dear. I could've done that.

FRANCES: It's no trouble. I've turned on the radio.

FRANK: Thank you, my dear.

FRANCES *goes to join* SAUL. FRANK *enters the cottage and settles himself into his reclining chair, operating the footrest expander mechanism several times. It still fascinates him. The radio has warmed up and is playing the latter part of Mozart's G Minor Quintet.*

SAUL: Welcome back. How is he?

FRANCES: He seems a lot better today, but I'm afraid he had a bad night.

SAUL: Was he coughing a lot?

FRANCES: Yes.

SAUL: His heart's too weak to clear the congestion from his lungs.

FRANCES: Saul, be truthful. Is he getting near the end?

SAUL: Yes.

FRANCES: Does he know that?

SAUL: I'm sure he does.

FRANCES: The pain in his back isn't lumbago, is it?

SAUL: No. It's referred pain from the heart. It's a bit like an exhausted runner forcing himself uphill but knowing that he's soon going to have to stop.

Up in the cottage the Quintet comes to an end. FRANK *seizes his paper and pencil.*

ANNOUNCER: [*voice-over*] That was the G Minor Quintet, Köchel 516, by Mozart—

FRANK: Yes. I know that.

ANNOUNCER: [*voice-over*] Played by the Amadeus Quartet—

FRANK: I thought so.

ANNOUNCER: [*voice-over*] With Cecil Aronowitz.

FRANK: Who? Speak more clearly, damn you. Speak up!

> FRANK *sighs in an irritated manner and puts down his pencil in disgust. He suddenly slumps back into his chair.*

ANNOUNCER: [*voice-over*] We will continue this concert with the Vivaldi Concerto in E Minor for Bassoon, played by the Chamber Orchestra of the Saar, conducted by Karl Ristenpart.

> *The music starts.*

SCENE TWENTY

FRANK is still in his chair, but has been straightened to an upright position. FRANCES, tear-streaked but resolute, reads a letter to SAUL and FREDDY.

FRANCES: No tears, no flowers, no priests, no piety, no headstones, and the first thing you all must do is to drink a full magnum of champagne.

SAUL: I'll go and get one.

FRANCES: No, it's all right.

> FRANCES *goes to the refrigerator and takes out a magnum.*

He always planned ahead.

> FREDDY *opens the bottle as* FRANCES *gets the glasses.*

Oh. He left this envelope for you, Saul.

> SAUL *opens it and takes out a ten-dollar note. He reads the message written on the accompanying notepaper.*

SAUL: Dear Saul. Here is your ten dollars. I'm afraid I can't offer you a rematch, but I think as a gentleman you should have offered me odds, as according to statistics you had a much better prognosis than I did. I'd appreciate it if you and Freddy would help Frances through all the arrangements which are listed separately in envelopes number three, three A and four. Will you thank Frances for the happy years she has given me and apologise to her sincerely for the miserable years I have given her. Tell her she would be well advised to travel south to her family before she gets caught up in the misfortunes of any other old crocks around the district. Regards, Frank.

FRANCES: He used to say that for all his faults he was damn well worth a magnum.

FREDDY: [*solemnly*] And so he was. Let's drink to that.

They drink the champagne. Suddenly the expanding footrest on the reclining chair, which has been on full extension, collapses back to its rest position under the weight of FRANK's *legs.* FRANCES, SAUL *and* FREDDY *jump with shock.*

SAUL: My God. I thought for a second that the old boy had come back. Much as I loved him I couldn't have taken another three years.

FRANCES: [*smiling despite herself*] Let's go out into the sunlight.

They take their glasses and move out into the garden. FRANCES *turns on the radio just as she leaves. It is playing Bach's Brandenburg Concerto Number Three. The music swells as they walk out into the sunlit garden.*

SAUL: Do you think you will go back down to your family?

FRANCES: No, I think somehow that I'll go travelling further north.

After a long pause, FRANK *rises from his chair and comes down to participate in the final bows with the rest of the cast.*

THE END

www.ingramcontent.com/pod-product-compliance
Lightning Source LLC
Chambersburg PA
CBHW050024090426
42734CB00021B/3409